Cyberbullying Crash Course:
Protect Your Kids from Cyberbullies, Cyber Violence, and Digital Peer Pressure

Bjorn Beam

Cyberbullying Crash Course:
Protect Your Kids from Cyberbullies,
Cyber Violence, and Digital Peer
Pressure

ISBN: 978-1-7342673-2-7 (Paperback)

First printing edition 2019.

www.SecuritySquad.org

For anyone living in the darkness of bullying

there is help

Table of Contents

Introduction

Bullying has been around since humans started to associate in communities, tribes, and nomadic settlements. It's innate that some tribe members try to pick on weaker tribe members, stemming from the *survival of the fittest* theorized by Charles Darwin. That's why it is so vital that we help victims of bullying while also changing the conversation to make bullying seem less appealing to the natural bullies of the world.

When bullying happens in person, it's obvious. A fight on the playground is reported, hopefully, to the principal, who then puts the bully in detention. The bully's parents are contacted, the bully is reprimanded, and justice is sometimes served.

Unfortunately, in this digital age, bullying is no longer as noticeable. Since the average teen spends more than nine hours per day online, signifying a massive switch from in-person communication to technology-based communication, a new form of bullying has arisen.[1] This form of online bullying, known as *cyberbullying*, cannot be seen or heard the way traditional bullying can. Many parents cannot detect it. There are no bruises on the face or scuff marks on the knees or calls from the principal. In fact, with cyberbullying, many of the victims' classmates might not even know it's happening.

Cyberbullying is an alarming development in our technological world. Sure, we are more connected and things are more convenient, but what about the dark side of human nature that is now exposed? We must be able to see what is going on behind closed doors to address it. Cyberbullying makes it incredibly hard for parents, educators, and teachers to know what's being said or done through direct messages, emails, etc.

And that is not to say that cyberbullying stops at kids. Plenty of adults are cyberbullied through dating apps, chat rooms, social media threads, and the posting of unwanted content, like in *photo extortion*. This problem does not just stop at cyberbullying; it also extends to *cyberhate*, where people are targeted because of their religious beliefs, skin color, sexual orientation, or political views.

We wish we could tell you this new age of cyberbullying will go away, but the reality is much different. It will only escalate unless we all become more vigilant and proactive. What needs to change is our awareness, attitude, and mindset toward it. Knowing it is here and prevalent, you and your family can prepare for what's out there. You can have chats, check-ins, and educational sessions in which you make your kids or students aware of forms of cyberbullying. As an educator, you can also set up an anonymous system whereby students can report cyberbullies to districts without being labeled as snitches.

We urge you to make the topic of cyberbullying less taboo. Cyberbullying is real, it is detrimental to human health (leading to some senseless suicides countrywide), and it's powerful. The more we keep the topic hushed, the more power these cyberbullies wield. We must understand the root causes and drivers of cyberbullying. We must use a triad approach: prevent, protect, and pursue. Understanding the motivations of cyberbullies may reveal a more sophisticated approach to combating them. Building an environment for kids to come forth and feel safe builds trust and understanding of what a community of acceptance, without cyberbullying, would mean. However, finally, bullies must understand that their actions will be met with repercussions that match their severity. And it's especially crucial that they fear a run-in with the law due to students reporting their activities to parents and teachers. There are legal implications for cyberbullying, and that must not be forgotten by all parties when we approach this complex societal problem. We must work to educate ourselves, our educators, and our politicians so no stone is left unturned. We must create a society in which victims feel safe to come forward and talk, and we must have laws that understand how to protect people and classify and prosecute this type of hate.

Together, we can all make this change. It starts with familiarizing yourself with digital peer pressure.

Let's begin.

CHAPTER 1

What Is Cyberbullying?

Mallory Grossman was a normal twelve-year-old girl with a loving family. But in October 2016, something changed. Mallory's mood darkened. She developed chronic headaches, and she frequently begged to stay home from school. Her mother, Dianne, was alarmed, as any parent would be. Was her daughter just experiencing the typical emotional ups and downs of the modern tween? Was she showing symptoms of an illness? Sadly, it was something worse: Mallory was being cyberbullied.

Through texts, Snapchat, and Instagram, several of Mallory's classmates told her that she was a loser and that she had no friends. They even suggested that she kill herself. Disturbed by what she'd learned, Dianne went to school authorities. They assured her they were investigating the incidents. Dianne even went to one of the bullies' parents, who brushed her off as though it was just harmless teenage fun.

But this wasn't harmless teenage fun for Mallory. At just twelve years old, she took her own life. Her family was devastated and desperate for answers. In August 2017, the Grossmans filed a lawsuit for negligence against the Rockaway School District.[2] The lawsuit could bring justice for Mallory, and it could help draw attention to cyberbullying and its very real impacts. It's a discussion we should all be having.

There is no way to sugarcoat it. Cyberbullying is a real, massive problem in our world today. About 34 percent of teens admit they have been cyberbullied, with 17 percent stating it has happened in the last thirty days. That figure is double what was uncovered in 2007, which indicates it will only increase.[3]

Even more alarming, 87 percent of teens admit they have seen cyberbullying occur online. Whether they have done something to stop it or not is another question.[4]

Here are some cold, hard numbers:

- 95 percent of teens are connected to the internet.[5]
- 85 percent of teens use social media.[6]
- 69 percent of people report having done something abusive toward others online.[7]
- 15 percent of people admit they have cyberbullied someone else online.[8]
- Over 50 percent of LGBT students have been cyberbullied.[9]
- 36 percent of girls have reported being cyberbullied, while 26 percent of boys have reported being cyberbullied.[10]

We could go on and on with disturbing statistics that indicate this form of bullying is not going away. The more pervasive our consumer technology becomes, from smartphones and watches to even potential holograms and completely online education systems, the more opportunity these bullies will have to wield technology in the wrong way. And so far, our legal system has failed to uniformly keep up with the bullies and the latest tech advancements, so protections against cyberbullying aren't very promising. Countries around the world have made varying degrees of strides in forming laws to deal with cyberbullying. However, here in the United States, each state deals with bullying differently through a mixture of laws and policies, and at the federal level, there's no law that explicitly addresses cyberbullying.[1112] It's only covered by federal law when it happens to overlap with other policies about harassment. With technology growing exponentially and lax or inconsistent protections in place, cyberbullying will continue to flourish.

But before we dive into the more nuanced aspects of cyberbullying, let's first consider its official definition.

The Definition of Cyberbullying

Cyberbullying is "bullying that takes place over digital devices such as cellphones, computers, and tablets, which includes, but is not limited to, SMS and text message, social media, forum, online gaming, any other app that allows people to view, participate, and share content" (StopBullying.gov and the National Crime Prevention Center).[1314]

These agencies classify cyberbullying as a more significant threat than physical, in-person bullying. This is because it occurs 24/7, it is more permanent since information is released onto the internet, and it's difficult to spot. Cyberbullying can occur through any means of communication, making traditional approaches to harassment challenging to defeat. There is no cap to the amount of hate and bullying that one can put out there, other than the amount of time they have. And with so many mediums one can use to bully, its grasp on its victims feels never-ending. The potential is limitless, completely silent and hard to spot, and hurtfully damaging by attacking students' emotions, mental health, and happiness.

Cyberbullying is also incredibly easy. All the bully needs is an internet connection. They don't even need their own phone—they can walk to the library in town, sit down, and use the desktop computer to wreak havoc on the world. With just five to ten minutes of internet connection per week, this person has the potential to pretend to be someone else and post hurtful comments or stories to start rumors or harass someone on social media.

12

Therefore, cyberbullying is free and highly attainable. Anyone can do it.

Where Are People Cyberbullied?

If cyberbullying is happening at all times, right under our noses, let's start by stating where it most commonly occurs. If we can pinpoint its launch point, we can be more effective in containing it in the future:

1. **Social Media Platforms:**
   Instagram is the largest cyberbullying social media platform in existence right now. Accordingly, 42 percent of cyberbullying occurs on Instagram, 37 percent occurs on Facebook, 31 percent occurs on Snapchat, 12 percent occurs on WhatsApp, 10 percent occurs on YouTube, and 9 percent occurs on Twitter.[15] Social media makes it incredibly easy to cyberbully through private, direct messaging features, comments, shares on posts, and photo extortion through the posting and sharing of private content. Since social media is entirely free and easy to download to any device, everyone is on it—but that includes the cyberbullies. With social media, these bullies can attack a person, publicly, in just a few minutes, and it has the potential to reach thousands of people. When something results in high engagement within the first few seconds of posting to Instagram, the app considers it "valuable content" that it then exponentially pushes to more users. You get the picture.

2. **Email:**

   This might seem like an odd place to cyberbully, since we typically associate email with adults emailing coworkers, clients, etc. However, email is very popular among teens and children, with the Pew Research Center reporting that 64 percent of teens use email to communicate with their friends.[16] With just a single click, a bully can send private information to large groups all at once, creating lists of recipients that will see the content forever. When an email is sent, the sender can do nothing to "un-send" it. It is permanent, forever.

3. **Texting:**

   Since teens are buried in their phones, they do, of course, use texting to take down their victims. Most students today have cellphones. According to the latest research, the average age a kid receives a phone is ten. Therefore, by middle school, every single student has a cellphone, which is most commonly a smartphone.[17] By creating texting groups, students can send images and videos to dozens of people at once. Again, once the text is sent, it cannot be un-sent. The content is forever.

4. **Instant Messaging:**

   Many teens will go for instant messaging over texting today. Whether it's Facebook Messenger, WhatsApp, or the direct message channel on Instagram, these streams are more "private" than public posting. This is where cyberbullies can privately harass, impersonate someone (catfish), or personally attack the victim and chip away at their mental health. Parents cannot readily see this happening, which is what makes it so appealing to the bullies.

There are also chat rooms (although not typical for teens), new apps like TikTok, and other channels where cyberbullying can occur. You will find cyberbullying through all social media platforms and their corresponding direct messaging features, text, and email.

CHAPTER 2

The Main Causes of Cyberbullying

Recognizing that cyberbullying is here to stay prompts the question of why it is so popular in the first place. Yes, technology has made cyberbullying possible, and, yes, there will always be those bad humans in every batch—but what about the large number of children and adults who would otherwise not engage in deviant conduct in everyday life?

Is there something alluring about cyberbullying? Can you find yourself in the act by accident, unable to stop?

Before we look at the different kinds of cyberbullying, let's first look at the leading causes.

Revenge

We were all kids once, and we know being in school can be difficult sometimes. Kids make fun of other kids, point out differences, bully kids who are not as smart as their peers, or make fun of those that go through puberty earlier than others. When this happens to a kid, naturally, they want to seek revenge. They could cope with the situation in healthier ways, or they could pick up their phone and get their satisfaction instantly.

It is common for many victims of bullying to want to retaliate for the pain inflicted on them.[18] When this happens, the retaliating victim is referred to as a *bully-victim*. They feel justified in seeking revenge because they were attacked first. They have been targeted and made to feel bad, so in their minds, the perpetrator deserves it in return.

We've all had someone make us feel terrible in front of others. We dream of telling that person what we really think. This is especially true if the person has been irritating us for years (like a relative or close friend).

Since the bully-victim feels that they do not have the power to defend themselves physically from the bully or cannot find adults willing to listen to their problems, the bully-victim sees little escape from this victimization cycle. These bully-victims commonly go after the bully directly online or target their closest friends to bring them down slowly.

Justification

In a cyberbully's head, they often believe the victim deserves it. There are many hierarchies in school settings. Let's say a popular girl goes home and starts to be bullied by a group of other girls. These girls could be the "less cool girls" that have joined together to make this one popular girl feel terrible. Or just one girl could target another girl known to be smart and successful. Jealous of her success, cyberbullying is an easy way for the student to get what she wants.

When there is justification in the person's mind for cyberbullying, they do not feel any guilt. With no guilt in the equation, things can get ugly quickly. This thought process is standard in dehumanizing someone to justify one's actions cognitively. Once the person is a "lesser" or "deserves it," then our normal human understandings of pain and sympathy fall to the wayside.

The bully's justification gives them emotional distance from the victim and creates a lack of empathy. Research shows that a lack of empathy can lead to destructive behavior, especially if the person lacking empathy doesn't have any other outlets to express themselves or keep busy.[19]

Boredom

Although this is not by any means a justification for ruining another's life, often, cyberbullies are home alone, bored, looking for entertainment. Remember when you used to open the phone book and call random numbers, telling them that their refrigerator was running? This is the same concept, except with our technology today, it can get much nastier.

Cyberbullying is also easy to do, even under parental supervision. If a child's parents don't let them go over to their friend's house, the child can wreak havoc online right from their room. It's an easy way to get the attention they are craving.

And if the bully lacks empathy, the abundance of free time creates a perfect storm for them to do destructive things. A 2011 article from the *Independent* reported that people who lack empathy could avoid hurting others if they have productive ways to spend their time. If they have passions—activities in which they can channel their energy—they can avoid cruel acts. But boredom is the exact opposite, giving the bully time and space to go after an unsuspecting victim.

Peer Pressure

We all regret a thing or two we said or did in school when our friend circle was watching. Peer pressure can make students do some pretty crazy things, including cyberbullying. Kids can be pressured to join a group designed to target one person. Although they might not feel good about it, they still want to be "cool" and liked, even if that means hurting someone else. Social status can be everything in school, which is why kids will cave to the pressure, not realizing what it's doing to the person on the receiving end. (The Netflix show *13 Reasons Why* does a good job depicting what happens when everyone caves to peer pressure in targeting a student.)

Normalcy

Cyberbullying is not an anomaly today. More than half of students are engaged in it, have been bullied, or know people doing it. Therefore, there is this sense of "everyone is doing it." With that kind of groupthink, kids feel less restrained when they engage in it since everyone else is doing it too. Not feeling alone, the single actor or lone wolf can be very dangerous in the long run.

Power Play

The politics of power start to emerge in kids as young as seven or eight. There will always be those kids on the playground that take charge, getting other kids to do their bidding. Well, that power-hungry feeling is alive and well in teens and, of course, adults, which is what makes cyberbullying so appealing. Using the internet, kids can perpetuate relational aggression and mean behavior, spreading rumors and gossip to take down a perceived competitor. This power play can make the kids feel that they have isolated the threat, so they no longer have to worry about it the next day in school.

But what about the dynamics of the world around these students? It can be easy for us to think our adult world does not impact the development process of our children. Yet as we all know, it is a very elementary reflection of our political system and spectrum today. Children mirror the realities around them. When they see the hatred, violence, and confrontation in our society on TV, in the home, or from political leaders, they normalize these behaviors as reflections of what society should be. It's just that none of us want to see younger and younger kids engaging in such behavior. This does not mean you should lock your TV away and live in a bunker, but it does mean you should take action in your daily life to explain the world around you to your kids. If we all lead by example, we might be surprised by what follows.

Assumed Secrecy

Cyberbullies and trolls know it's hard to detect their activity today, and they love the secrecy. [i]They believe they won't be caught, which is why they exhibit their worst behavior. We all do this to a certain extent. Remember your summer high school job flipping burgers or lifeguarding, or even in your job today, as is replicated on shows like *The Office*—when the boss isn't around, what do you do? Slack off, of course! It is human nature to take the path of least resistance while enjoying the secrecy of doing it and not getting caught. There is a thrill, a neurological response that triggers a rush with this "life on the edge."

Well, with cyberbullying, it's as if the boss is always off. When there is no boss, the darker side of human nature flourishes. The checks and balances of society are missing to demonstrate the right path. A new reality is created where it is the bully and his or her keyboard. They are the maker and destroyer of dreams. What could stop this type of power?

---

[i] I added trolls here because while not fully interchangeable with cyberbullying, it highlights the range in which bullies can operate. Bullies can be overt or covert with their attacks. Anonymous emails or email-altering software can obscure where the messages came from.

Parenting Failure

Last, there are those characterologically cold type of kids that lack empathy.[20] Whether it's a genetic or mental condition[ii] or parenting failures, these kids are going to be ruthless with the internet in their hands. Their parents may be abusive or neglectful, and the kids may have learned unacceptable societal behaviors from living at home. Or they have witnessed older siblings exhibiting such behavior. Kids pick up habits through <u>observational learning</u>, also known as the *monkey see, monkey do* model of child behavior.[21] This starts at an early age. So if a child watches a parent or sibling bully others or shows a general lack of respect for other people, they learn this behavior too. They've seen it in action, and they have deemed it appropriate. In these cases, the bullies have parents or other adults who did not step in and teach their kids about empathy and compassion for their fellow peers.

These kids could go to great lengths to tear down others because cognitively, they see nothing wrong with it. Additionally, this type of mindset can lead to other societal problems down the road.

Can We Prevent These Causes?

Although not all of these causes can be addressed, like the innate human struggle for power, parents can be more proactive in teaching their children about both being bullies and being bullied. Sharing with kids that their cyberbullying can be reported and that it is a crime to engage in such activity can provide a new sense of perspective in their minds.

[ii] Caveat: I am not saying one is genetically or mentally predisposed to be a bully. I am saying that certain environmental and biological circumstances could lead to this emotion being manifested differently.

And addressing the boredom angle is also possible, building in new activities and engagement each night, so children are not upstairs on their phones for hours and hours. The longer they sit on their phones, the more tempting the cyberbullying rabbit hole can seem. Create real positive social situations for them to engage with their peers. These real human connections will show them that there are real people on the other side of these devices and that there is a world beyond the digital.

Proactive parents, teachers, and administrators are certainly a start.

Next, we will go through the five most common forms of cyberbullying today, breaking down what they look like, how to spot them, and how to potentially eradicate them.

First up, the most popular form of cyberbullying: cyber harassment.

CHAPTER 3

Cyber Harassment

Cyber harassment arguably is the easiest and most deployed form of cyberbullying online today. Succeeding in cyber-harassment does not involve too much thought/technological aptitude. That is why so many students succumb to this form of bullying: it's within reach, it's attainable, and everyone else is doing it, right?

Let's look at an official definition.

What Is Cyber Harassment?

Cyber harassment involves sending offensive and threatening messages via instant messaging, SMS, or any other form of communication to affect a target directly. Just one person can wage the bullying, or an entire group of students can conspire to gang up on one person. When this occurs, multiple people can send out thousands of messages at once. The limitlessness of technology is detrimental in this instance.

A cyber harassment victim could receive repeated and unpleasant messages every hour, every thirty minutes, or even every minute, depending on how many people are involved.

What Does Cyber Harassment Look Like?

Cyber harassment takes place through varying forms, and these forms have subtle differences in their manifestation and prevention. Let's delve deeper into the actual forms of cyber harassment:

- **Instant messaging:** There are a lot of instant messaging portals today. From GChat to Facebook Messenger, to Instagram DMs, students and teens have many options if they want to target a victim. With instant messaging, they can send repeated messages, they can create groups and then post defamatory content to the one hundred plus people in the group, and they can even make anonymous accounts that make it impossible to track who is sending the content. There's a constant stream of harassment that's practically impossible to stop, as demonstrated in the following example:

    > Diva7712: Loser, you should stop showing up at school.
    > Flower**11: What r u talking about?
    > Diva7712: You should just kill yourself. No one likes you.
    > Flower**11: Why don't you just leave me alone?
    > Diva7712: You need to be put in your place.

    The goal is often to target, embarrass, and silence the victim. This type of event can be a broader planned cyberbullying effort or an event-driven attack. An event-based attack in this instance could be Flower**11 talking about how a birthday party last weekend was great, which Diva7712 didn't go to. Regardless of whatever the exact trigger is, the bully's targeted message and subsequent escalation can have a crippling effect on the intended target.

- **Rumors/threats:** Rumors and gossip have been around since the beginning of time. However, with the internet, now a student can make up a rumor and blast it in just seconds. This can include posting embarrassing information, contact information (doxing), and other strips of text across Facebook, Twitter, and Instagram. This can also include actual threats. For example, the FBI began monitoring threatening social media posts from Anthony Elonis toward his wife, who'd he recently separated from.[22] His posts included graphic descriptions about inflicting bodily harm. Though rumors and threats happen online, there could be real-world implications that are quite scary.[iii][23]

- **Warning wars:** Many apps, like Instagram, have a report button so you can flag inappropriate content or behavior. However, improper use of these buttons can also create conflict and frustration. Kids will get together and all flag a particular post or account to have someone kicked off of a social media app. Even organizations can wage war on content they don't like, although it doesn't violate an app's policies. This is simply a method of intimidation and troublemaking. For example, in 2012, a conservative group was accused of flagging pro-gay-rights Facebook pages because they didn't align with their beliefs.[24] This example and many others prove that the flagging system is easy to weaponize. Although the apps are trying to be better about this, it's still part of their system that is hard for them to

---

[iii] In late 2010, Anthony Elonis was arrested, charged, and convicted on four counts for violating a federal anti-threat statute because of threats made against his ex-wife, coworkers, a kindergarten class, local police, and an FBI agent. The US Supreme Court overturned the charges, claiming there was insufficient intent to commit the crimes.

override. Manual review is limited to case-by-case bases, and AI-based flag reviews are still years behind where they need to be to fully operate like a human eye.

- **Text attacks:** Text message attacks usually entail thousands of texts that are sent to a victim over a short period. These attacks can essentially make the victim's phone unusable, overwhelming the person with negative and mean comments repeatedly. This not only causes emotional distress, but also can rack up the cellphone bill quickly, getting the victim in trouble with their parents simultaneously. These records from the Yoknapatawpha County Sheriff's Department offer a detailed look at just how disruptive and troubling text attacks can be.[25]

Cyberbullies have creative imaginations, which is why they can mix any form of harassment listed above to really attack their victims. Sometimes they will leverage two or three types of harassment simultaneously to try to inundate the target. When this happens, it can escalate to offline confrontation when the attacker's identity is known.

Offline Escalation

When harassment includes *meeting spots* or an anonymous attacker accidentally lets their identification slip through in the attacks, this can sometimes lead to offline escalation. Here, online bullying turns into offline bullying, although this can lead to highly dangerous fights and confrontations during or after school.

If you notice your child is getting into more fights in school than ever before, it may be fueled by cyberbullying you can't see. That's why it's so important to talk to your child and ask them about what's going on. Even if you do not see physical fights, remain vigilant for rapid mood changes in students. This could be caused by other issues, but in any case, it should not be neglected.

Outing

Outing is a subsection of cyber harassment, specifically geared toward members of the LGBT community. When information is obtained to indicate that a student may be gay, bisexual, or questioning, the cyberbully will spread that information around the internet, outing the person before the person makes their own choice to do so. (This can be photo extortion as well if actual media of homosexual activity is obtained.)

Outing is one of the most prominent headlines regarding teen suicides today.[26] Tennessee teen Channing Smith and New Jersey teen Tyler Clementi both took their lives after being bullied online for being gay and/or wearing nail polish. In Tyler's case, which took place back in 2010, his roommate cyberbullied him by covertly filming and broadcasting Tyler's dorm room hookups.

Nine-year-old Jamel Myles from Denver killed himself after his classmates bullied him online for being gay. After he wore false fingernails on the first day of school, students took to messaging apps to spread rumors that he was gay, inspiring him to take his life just a few days later.

Nigel Shelby was an Alabama high school freshman who took his life after both classmates and unsympathetic school administrators told him being gay was a "choice." Some deputies in the area even left comments on posts online, contributing to the bullying that inspired the student to take his life. The deputy sheriff in Alabama's Madison County was placed on leave once these social media comments were unearthed. This is why it is so crucial for parents, educators, and law enforcement to take all of these claims seriously. The stakes are too high not to pay attention.

It's no surprise, then, that about two million LGBTQ youth contemplate suicide every year in the United States.[27] And a 2019 study confirmed that about 25 percent of all young adolescent suicides in children ages twelve to fourteen are by LGBTQ youth.[28]

Legislation

Right now, there is a variety of laws or pieces of legislation in place to try to prevent the hardship caused by cyberbullying and cyber harassment. The Tyler Clementi Higher Education Anti-Harassment Act would require colleges and universities to establish policies that prohibit harassment, while also helping schools to create anti-cyberbullying programs.[29]

There is also the Tyler Clementi Foundation, which works every day to help teens thinking about suicide reconsider their options. The foundation hosts the Tyler Clementi Upstander Pledge, which is an online pledge against online and offline bullying and harassment.

Should You Worry About Cyber Harassment?

In the coming chapters, we will look at how you can assess whether your child is being bullied, the side effects of such cyberbullying, and how you can prevent it.

But what we can tell you now is that you absolutely should worry about cyber harassment. Given the widespread nature of such activity, it's safe to say your child or student will be a target for defamation at one time or another.

Now it's time to move onto a more "creative"—and potentially lethal—form of cyberbullying: catfishing.

CHAPTER 4

Catfishing

To highlight what catfishing is, let us bring you to a story of a girl pretending to be someone she was not.

DeAnna Hall was just fifteen years old when she joined a Britney Spears chat room.[30] There, she used the name Mandi, lied about her age, as she was underage, and met an older guy from the Netherlands. She gave him her real phone number. They spoke on the phone daily and developed a connection. Soon, the man from the chat room wanted to visit Mandi. To maintain her cover, she developed a bizarre lie about getting into a car accident and losing her memory. Eventually, she was unable to keep up the lie, and she told him the truth. This might seem silly and frivolous (and downright strange) to some, but it's actually an example of catfishing. While this story was fairly innocent regarding DeAnna Hall's intentions, it can be extremely manipulative and dangerous.

When we are discussing catfishing, we are not talking about the fish native to the Southeastern region of the United States. When we say *catfishing*, we are referring to a specific form of cyberbullying that involves pretending to be someone else to get someone to admit something, open up, share information, or share contact information/addresses, etc. This can be done by creating or stealing another person's persona and using that to build trust with an unsuspecting individual. Kids can become catfishing victims in two ways—they could be lured or tricked by someone who's pretending to be someone they're not, or their identity could be stolen and used in a separate catfishing scheme.

Unfortunately, catfishing has become somewhat romanticized in our lives today. Why? MTV created a highly popular show called _Catfish: The TV Show_. This show has a limited scope, often focusing on romantic relationships that started online, like the example described above. The show's hosts team up with the catfishing victim to get their story. They investigate the catfishing suspect to figure out their true identity. Then, they track down the suspect and arrange a confrontation between the suspect and their catfishing victim. Most episodes end with a dramatic showdown in which the suspect reveals why they catfished in the first place.

With TV crews and professionals involved, this kind of discovery may not be dangerous. However, when a student goes to find the truth on their own, and no cameras are rolling, they could be unknowingly going to a pedophile or sex offender's home. Furthermore, the narrow focus of _Catfish: The TV Show_ paints catfishing as a purely romantic tactic, when, in reality, it can be used in many different ways.

Catfishing is something you should lose sleep over. It's real, it's terrifying, and it's persuasive. Kids at an early age have a tendency to believe what they are told. This is known as the _theory of the mind_. The theory holds that it takes several years through infancy and early childhood for children to learn and understand that people do not hold the same thoughts and feelings as they do. Therefore, they have to learn to interpret others' emotions and intentions, which are not always pure. Children continue to develop their understandings of what is real/fake and with hidden intentions well after age five.[31][32]

What Is Catfishing?

Catfishing is a form of online impersonation where a person chooses to pose as someone else and talk to the victim as a friend. It can be a forty-year-old man using pictures of a fifteen-year-old guy from a few states away, creating accounts, and pretending to be this person. Since there are volumes of content pieces per person on social media today, this man can download a hundred pictures of this actual, living, breathing student from across the country and pretend to be them. This is another reason it is so important to have strong privacy settings on your account, which I will discuss in my subsequent book. The whole world does not need to know your activities or see all your photos.

Once the catfishers set up the fake accounts, they start to chat. Many times, they target insecure girls that would be ecstatic to have a handsome young man messaging them. The catfishers begin to win their target's trust, having long, personal, intense talks with them into the night, complimenting them, and even calling them on the phone. They will, of course, never be able to FaceTime and risk exposing their actual identity.

This can go on for months. It can go on for so long that the victim truly believes they are in love and have found their soul mate. From countless days of chatting and bonding, they will come to trust this person. So when the person requests that they finally meet at a parking lot a few towns over, the victim may be more than willing to make it happen. In their head and heart, they feel like they really, truly know this person.

Now, not all catfishing is by online predators; there are many instances when it's done by insecure boys or girls looking to woo someone they are crushing on from afar. It can also be done by gay students hoping to get the attention of a crush of their same-sex that they know is not in the LGBTQ community. The bottom line is, it can be done by anyone and for any purpose.

Regardless of the reason for catfishing, the victim ends up hurt, betrayed, embarrassed, and crushed. They end up not being able to trust anyone, for anything. This type of lost trust can also be directed toward technology itself, leading to a loss of confidence in all forms of digital. Although the intentions might not be harmful in the case of a crush, catfishing is still something all parents need to be watching for—especially if your child asks to go meet up with an internet friend.

Online Predators

As of 2017, there are 86,137 registered sex offenders in the United States.[33] Additionally, with the rise of social media and messaging apps, the FBI warns that online sexual predators are on the rise, with many of them engaging in "sextortion" cases.[34] Catfishing students, they can get young girls to send inappropriate photos that they then use for personal pleasure, money, or sharing in illegal chat rooms.

Online predators know they can effectively reach their victims in the following places:

- **Social media:** Social media makes it easy to find a victim and start messaging them. Especially if the child's profile is public, child predators know how to find the quieter, more isolated or solitary students that are looking for affection and attention. They will start with just a message here and there across their social profiles, stimulating the student's interest.

- **Chat rooms:** Although many students do not go into chat rooms, there is still a segment of kids that will accidentally end up in these messaging rooms. When they are engaged and asked questions, their curiosity will increase. They'll log back on tomorrow just to see what's happening. It will escalate from there.

- **Dating apps:** Dating apps, especially gay dating apps, are a common place for predators to find their victims. They tend to target the questioning LGBTQ students, knowing they are vulnerable and looking to find out more about themselves.

In this impersonation form of cyberbullying, there a few keys ways bullies carry out their attacks:

- **Creating fake accounts:** Bored teenagers go onto Instagram or other apps and get a username that is very similar to the victim's username. They then upload their photos and pretend to be that person, sending rude or hurtful remarks to other kids in the class. They use the victim's image to cyberbully even more kids, without ever being accountable for what they have done. And even when the victim explains that it wasn't them, with the username to prove it, sometimes the damage has already been done. When you can't see who is behind the comments, how do you know who to trust?

- **Password recovery:** Students with an aptitude for technology can steal other students' passwords and log into their accounts. They can then pretend to be the account holder and use their victim's account to bully other individuals with comments that just can't be taken back.

- **Public smearing:** Once these individuals are in the accounts, they can change everything from the biography to the profile picture. They can upload embarrassing photos and make comments that are homophobic, racist, or sexually demeaning. This can actually get the student that owns the account in trouble with the school and the law.

- **Chat room impersonation:** The bully can also create an account for the victim on a site they have never visited, pretending to be them. They can go into child porn chat rooms and other illegal places, where they can release personal information and photos of the victim. This can make it easy for these perpetrators to target the victim on other social media sites, not knowing it wasn't actually them in the chat room.

With technology today, the sky is really the limit for online impersonation. For the students who are bored, it's exactly what they need to fill their entertainment requirements for the day.

The above examples are attacks that can be waged in just a few hours. However, catfishing is deeper than just these initial techniques. It can go on for weeks, if not months, and sometimes, even years. Catfishing is a new level of psychological manipulation and intimidation that can make it hard for the victim to come back to reality. The victim assumed that they could trust this person—does that mean their entire worldview is skewed?

Keeping an open communication channel with your kids is important for identifying if sexual predators have infiltrated their lives. If you see them messaging the same person or username on their phone, even at the dinner table, it's okay to ask who they are. Sex predation is a real problem in our world, and it will only get worse with the technology available today.

CHAPTER 5

Photo Extortion

As we previously touched on, photo extortion is a form of cyber harassment that can embarrass the victim beyond belief. Many students who have taken their own lives, as mentioned earlier in the book, did so once a video or photo of their private or sexual activity was distributed. However, photo extortion knows no bounds for sexual orientation, religion, or socioeconomic class. Let us not forget about the reach of revenge porn or hacks. Take a look at the Hollywood hacks that placed Jennifer Hudson and several other prominent Hollywood actors' private pictures all over the internet.[35]

People can easily say it was not them that released the photos or that their face was photoshopped onto these images, but the damage has already been done. An image has been created, and a reputation has been destroyed. With comments and statements, students can insist it wasn't them. Some people will believe them, but will that be enough to make life go back to normal?

There's no coming back from a photo. You cannot un-ring the bell. With photos, there is living, breathing, and physical evidence that someone did something. Photos and videos tell everyone viewing that this did indeed happen, it is real, and it is just waiting to be the new hot gossip in town.

The victim has nowhere to go, nowhere to hide. They feel so isolated and alone that they are willing to do terrible things. Sometimes, they take their own life.

What are explicit forms of photo extortion today?

- **Secret nude shots:** It's easy to hide a camera in the girls' locker room, snap some nude shots, and then do what you want with them. A cyberbully can also hide commercially available spy cameras in sensitive areas and take the photos themselves remotely, obviously accruing the content without permission. Then they can send the material around the internet.

- **Blackmailing:** Let's say a student (A) shared a sensitive photo with a former lover (B). Things went south and that former lover (B) now has the sensitive photo. The former lover (B) can use it to blackmail the student, threatening to make it public if they don't abide by certain rules. Additionally, a third party person could get it from the former lover (B) and then hang it over the student (A) or the former lover (B). In any variation you can come up with, blackmail is used as a tool of threat and intimidation.

- **Mass sext emails:** Once a cyberbully gets their hands on sensitive content, they can blast out emails or texts with the photos, making the content permanent forever. There is no way to undo it.

- **Photo-sharing sites:** Cyberbullies can post the photos in photo-sharing apps and chat rooms, giving them to other people—potentially child molesters.

- **Slut-shaming:** The cyberbully can post the photo by themselves, stating that the victim is a "slut" and a "whore" for taking the photo in the first place. Students can chime in in the comments and agree.

Video Extortion

Video extortion takes the same form as photo extortion, except with video content. Video content can be illegally recorded in a room where two students are engaging in sexual activity. Or the students can willingly film the video together, with one of the participants sharing it with other students unbeknownst to the victim.

Videos can be sent through apps, emails, and other social media sites effortlessly. Once these videos are posted, they are permanent, which can make this form of cyberbullying very stressful for the victim.

Explicit forms of video shaming can include the following:

- Setting up a bullying incident, like slapping or tripping a kid, while having someone else positioned with their phone to film it. Then the kid takes the video and blasts it to everyone in the school to embarrass the victim.
- Recording an embarrassing video and posting it on YouTube so the entire world can view the content.
- Sharing videos through mass email chains.
- Causing a problem that makes the other person upset or emotional and then recording their response. This can happen over video chat, FaceTime, etc.
- Coaxing the victim into recording an inappropriate video and then using the video to blackmail them.

What About Photoshopping?

There are some highly advanced photo editing tools out there today. We've all seen the before and after examples of models in magazines. Bodies can be altered, skin color can be changed, and backgrounds can be changed. Therefore, some students with exceptional photoshopping abilities can take an innocuous photo of the victim and turn it into something else.

The result is a photo that looks believable, which makes it nearly impossible for the victim to refute the claims. This can take just a few hours and some serious photo editing precision.

The best thing you can do is sit down with your child or student and explain that under no circumstances should sensitive content ever be sent to a friend or lover through the internet that they would not want the whole world to see. They should also be aware of recording equipment in places like locker rooms, which is why it doesn't hurt to check around first before undressing.[iv]

And the same thing goes for using the bathroom. If there are purses or items left in the stall that shouldn't be there, inspect them to ensure there is no camera positioned to film them while using the toilet. (Unfortunately, there is a fetish following for this kind of content.) Coming from an intelligence background, I would advise reporting any unattended bags to security, as domestic terrorism is a more pressing safety issue than spy cameras. In either case, you are training your students and children to observe their surroundings.

[iv] Commercially available spy cameras have become extremely sophisticated and difficult to spot to even with the most trained eyes. It is disturbing this is where were have come to in life, but you do not want to induce paranoia, with kids being afraid to enter a bathroom or locker room.

Next, we will look at the creation of entire websites, blogs, and polls aimed at the victim.

CHAPTER 6

Websites, Blogs, and Polls

This is a more advanced form of cyberbullying, one that involves some serious time and attention. Beyond harassing through direct messaging portals and other places, cyberbullies can go online and make entire websites, landing pages, and blogs dedicated to their victims. This form of bullying requires some website aptitude and ability. However, many of the website programs today come with very easy templates that can make it possible for anyone to create a website.

If the cyberbully makes an entire website dedicated to the victim, then it's safe to say they're obsessed with tearing them down. Often, if the bully has been bullied by a person, in person, for years, then the hate and hurt have built up. The victim will do whatever it takes to ensure they get "justice."

A website is a convenient place to aggregate everything they want to share with the public, ensuring the target is completely embarrassed.

David Knight of Burlington, Ontario, had no idea a website about him existed.[36] The site featured lots of false information—it claimed he was gay, dirty, and a pedophile. The site also invited others to join in and leave comments. The activity spiraled out of control, with site users sending him hurtful emails about the reasons they didn't like him. David soon learned about the site but didn't allow it to affect his self-worth or lead him to harm himself. But not every kid is as resilient as David. Cyberbullying websites can be a real detriment to kids' mental health and well-being.

Cyberbully Websites

What exactly appears on these targeted websites?

- **Information:** Perhaps it's personal information that was meant to be a secret, or contact information people can use to start texting the victim. Whatever it is, sensitive information can be listed and plastered across any website, for anyone to access. Often bullies will include contact information, like an email address and a phone number, so groups of cyberbullies can get together and bombard their phone (as we mentioned earlier in the book).

- **Photos:** These photos can be illegal and embarrassing photos taken unbeknownst to the person. Or they can be photos they willingly posted on their social media, with editing done to make them look terrible. This can make the victim feel poorly about themselves and their appearance.

- **Videos:** Video clips can be added as well. If there's a video of the victim falling or failing to stop the winning goal against the soccer team, that can play at the top of the website, creating a movement to make fun of the person.

- **Rumors:** Who says the information must be true and accurate? The cyberbully can make up blatant lies and post them all around the website. If they are really bored, they can fabricate false evidence to back up the rumors and gossip, creating completely unfounded stories. Often, cyberbullies will post homophobic slurs and claims.

It doesn't stop at just websites. There are also blogs (single-page or full-website blogs) the cyberbully can fill with embarrassing and false information about the victim. The blog can contain article after article claiming the victim did something they, in fact, did not. But when the article looks legitimate, all bundled and presented on a blog for the public to read, it can seem true.

Just think of our fake news problem today. When a headline graces social media coming from a seemingly reputable source, we assume it's true. There's a news article, so surely it's real. That same concept holds true for posting entire blogs targeted at someone.

And then there are polls. Instagram released a polling feature in Instagram Stories last year that enables users to take a poll from those scrolling through the Stories feed. Although this can be perfectly harmless, and valuable to businesses, it can also be incredibly hurtful to individuals.

Plenty of poll sites take just a few minutes to set up a poll and text or email it out to thousands of people. In the poll, these topics can be addressed:

- Who is the ugliest, fattest, or smelliest
- Who is the hottest among boys and girls (like the impetus of Mr. Zuckerberg's Facebook)
- Who has the best grades or the most accolades

When the poll makes its way back to the victim and they can see that hundreds of people have voted they are the fattest, smelliest, or ugliest when compared to others in their grade, they can feel completely sad and alone. They don't know where to turn. Can you imagine such a thing happening when you were in school?

Spyware

This is for the really advanced tech geniuses out there. Spyware is any unwanted software that infiltrates your computer to steal your data or sensitive information. Bullies have two options with spyware:

they can either make it themselves, which requires a serious amount of attention, or they can find malware and send it to the victim to try to mess with their phone and electronics.

1. **Creating the spyware:** Technology is becoming a more significant part of the curriculum in school today. Why? Our market demands it. Therefore, the basics of creating malicious software are becoming more attainable to students, which means they can essentially make their own hacking programs.

    They only need to mail or text out a link to dozens of people with some kind of deceptive message, implying that it will help people win something or money. When these unknowing victims click the link, they allow the virus to infiltrate their computer, which can enable the malware creator to do everything from steal passwords to see the individual through their computer camera.

2. **Sending the spyware:** A very small percentage of teens know how to make their own spyware. However, any regular teen can be an agent for an already existing malware virus or malware program. As a kid, I even remember seeing a program that would easily create Trojan horse viruses for you. This type of make-your-own Trojan horse has only improved in sophistication. All the person has to do is send it to the victim and hope he or she will open it. Many send deceptive malware messages to the person relentlessly until they finally open one up against their better judgment.

This is where cyberbullying and cybersecurity can overlap. This form of bullying can result in a cybersecurity breach detrimental to the targeted individual, their personal information, and even their family. As a parent or teacher, you can teach your kids about the act of cybersecurity and how to look for phishing emails. Some tips include the following:

- **Misspellings in the email.** Often, malware programs are made overseas, which means the creators don't have a fluent grasp of English.

- **Bogus email address.** If the email is about your Apple account but the sender's email is something crazy like Nina@theguardiansofthesea.com, it's not legitimate. If a company like Apple was actually trying to contact you, the email would be info@apple.com.

- **Aggression in the email or text body/subject.** Reputable companies don't threaten their consumers. Therefore, if an email is trying to tell you to do something immediately or else lose out on something else, it's probably fake. You can also update your malware detector software and email settings to try to filter out these kinds of correspondence.

Finally, we are on to the last form of popular cyberbullying today. It's something we all are possibly guilty of: trolling.

CHAPTER 7

Subtweeting & Trolling

This is a more nuanced form of cyberbullying. It's one that can slowly eat away at someone, although nothing explicitly "wrong" is being done in the interim. Trolling is in a gray legal area, and it does not violate the terms and services of our favorite social media apps. That's why it can be such a mean form of cyberbullying and one hard to pinpoint as a parent or teacher.

Trolling is the act of posting comments, content, and texts or tweets obviously alluding to someone, without saying their name.

Some examples include the following:

- A boyfriend breaks up with his girlfriend. She takes to Twitter to tweet: "Thank God that's over with. If he can't stack up to five inches, why even bother. Am I right, ladies?" It is clear the girlfriend is tweeting about her boyfriend and divulging very sensitive information about the boyfriend. The entire school will read it and know who she is referencing.

- Someone in a particular grade lives in a trailer park, while the rest of the school comes from an affluent background. Someone tweets or posts: "I understand living in a trailer park isn't easy, but my God, can't you still shower? Why do all poor people ALSO smell!?" Here, it's obvious the person is targeting the poor kid from the trailer park, while calling them smelly along the way. The tweet or post has the potential to go viral.

Subtweeting, *trolling*, and *vaguebooking* are all terms used to describe this behavior. Here's a quick overview of what these terms refer to:

1. **Subtweeting:** *Subtweeting* refers specifically to the activity that occurs on Twitter. This is when someone tweets about someone else without tagging them, but it's very obvious who they are tweeting about. The tweet has the potential to go viral if enough people re-tweet it, comment on it, or share it on their wall. A very famous example of subtweeting involves Kim Kardashian West.[37] In July 2016, she tweeted, "Wait, it's legit National Snake Day?!?!? They have holidays for everybody, I mean everything these days!" She followed it with several snake emojis. She didn't name the tweet's target, but anyone with even vague knowledge of pop culture at the time knew she was subtweeting Taylor Swift, with whom she was feuding about a disagreement over a lyric from Kanye West's song "Famous." Kardashian West was retweeted more than 225,000 times, adding fuel to a very public squabble and demonstrating the negative power of subtweeting.

2. **Trolling:** *Trolling* is a more general term that describes the type of bullying described as *subtweeting*, but on any social media site. It can occur on Facebook, Instagram, Pinterest, etc. Here, the person will comment under someone's post, shading them indirectly. Or they will write a caption under their own post clearly alluding to someone else. Or they might reenact a photo someone else posted, making fun of it in their post. Trolling is usually less targeted, making this more difficult to track down. Because of this, there is likely no

connection between the troll and the victim. The troll just wants to create pain and cause havoc.

3. **Vaguebooking:** *Vaguebooking* is a newer term in the world of cyberbullying, referring to any update on a social network that is intentionally vague. As the name implies, it relates primarily to Facebook, but it can happen on other sites. Examples could be, "I am SO angry right now," or "I am so confused right now, why?" or "I can't believe they did that to me." It gets people talking underneath the post, asking what is going on. This then gives the person a platform from which to slander the other person who made them sad, mad, or angry. From a victim standpoint, it's then easy to rally support around their cause and win sympathy from their fake or false explanations.

We have probably all trolled, vaguebooked, or subtweeted at one time or another. Humans want attention, they want to be felt sorry for, and they want to be on the winning side of the argument. It's just too easy to sign into these apps and make a case for why we have been wronged. Who doesn't want to hear other people say, "You are so right!"?

If you suspect a student is being subtweeted or trolled, it's essential to talk to them and encourage them to ignore the subtweets or get off of the app altogether. No one should have to endure such passive-aggressive comments every day. That's what makes trolling so dangerous—it may seem harmless in the interim, but it can accumulate, day after day.

Let's say some students get together and make a hashtag for an overweight student named Tim. Their hashtag is #TimtheBlimp. Every time Tim posts on social media, someone comments on the picture, "#TimtheBlimp." Hundreds of kids can get in on it. It creates this feeling of isolation that can make kids depressed, anxious, and suicidal. It can feel like the world is against them.

This is the very reason study after study has proven that social media apps harm young people's mental health.[38]

But in reality, your kid or student will not get off of social media. They want to be cool. We all do.

So what can you do? Next, we'll look at signs a kid is being cyberbullied, so you can be proactive in helping them.

CHAPTER 8

How to Know if Your Child Is Being Cyberbullied

For these next two chapters, we are breaking suggestions down by category: student and child. We believe the parent and teacher roles are entirely different, yet equally important, in identifying if a student or child is being cyberbullied. Children are not equipped to handle this kind of psychological manipulation on their own, which is why the adults in their lives must be vigilant at every turn.

Starting with parents, you know just how terrifying the concept of cyberbullying can be. It's a hidden entity that can steal your child from you, as thousands of families have lamented the suicides of young, confused, and isolated children.

That's why the first step to protecting your child is to identify if they are being cyberbullied. Some of these points will double for teachers as well, but let's begin from a parental perspective.

8 Signs Your Child Is Being Cyberbullied

Sign 1: Shows Signs of Nervousness Upon Receiving a Text/Message

If you notice your child appears nervous, anxious, panicked, or sweaty upon receiving a message on their phone, this can be an initial indication of cyberbullying. Whether it's at the dinner table, when watching TV as a family, or when tucking them into bed after they brush their teeth, children should not be wincing when they check their phone.

This is where common sense comes into the picture. Only you know your child, which means you should be able to tell if they seem uneasy or nervous. Look for body language cues or noticeable changes in mood after a message is received/opened, for example, a text message that prompts your child to ask if they can "go to bed early" tonight.

Sign 2: Makes Up Lies for Getting Out of School

Sure, every child pretends they are sick every now and then to get out of a test or some school project. But if you notice it becoming a habit, it could be a sign of something deeper.

This should be especially alarming if your child likes school/their friends at school and used to enjoy going to class every day.

This can also include signs of general uneasiness from the child about going to school or a distaste for school altogether and negative or vague responses when asked how they are liking school.

Sign 3: Defensive About Online Information

Again, you must exercise common sense here. Obviously, no teenager wants their parents to read their text messages. However, if you even glance over at the phone or ask who they are texting and they respond with anger and rage, this can be a sign of cyberbullying. Often, when children are cyberbullied, they become afraid of outing the bully for fear of making the threats worse.

Therefore, if the child is becoming increasingly defensive with their phone (sleeping with it in their bed), then they are possibly trying to hide something that makes them scared, embarrassed, and humiliated.

Don't forget about Stockholm syndrome, which is a psychological condition in which a hostage develops a psychological alliance with their captor during captivity. After a while, the bullying, insults, and demanding behavior starts to shape the victim's self-worth and connection to the bully. This can happen to your child via cyberbullying. Your child may not realize how evil the person on the other end is. If you suggest that, it might make your child draw away from you even further. Be gentle about asking for online information—you don't want to scare your child away. But ultimately, you are the adult paying for the phone bill.

Sign 4: Unexplained Anger/Fits After Using Phone or Internet

Echoing sign 1, do you notice your child emerging from their room, laptop, or phone in an irrationally angry state? Did they get off of the school bus happy, chipper, and normal, only to do a total 180 right before dinner?

It's not normal for kids to have such dramatic mood swings. Sure, teenagers can be moody, especially teenage girls—but to see them go from happy to downright miserably mean in just minutes can be a sign of something bigger than them.

Sign 5: Withdrawing from Family and Friends

When depression and anxiety wash over us, it can convince us to withdraw from friends and family. The voices in our heads can tell us we're a burden to everyone around us and would be better off not bothering anyone at all.

This same concept can result from cyberbullying. The continued loss of self-worth will build in the child as they internalize this external sentiment. After being told they are nothing repeatedly, your child can start to believe it and withdraw from you and their friends. It's a natural reaction to something they seemingly have no control over.

Sign 6: Health Ailments

It is no secret that mental stress and anguish can manifest physically in our bodies. Therefore, the burden of cyberbullying can make your child ill, and commonly causes:

- insomnia;
- depression;
- anxiety;
- stomachaches; or
- headaches.

Children are supposed to be healthy, vibrant, and thriving organic beings. They are not supposed to be living with migraines and sleeping problems that make them unenergetic. Therefore, if you notice your previously healthy child complaining about any one of these problems, it could be a sign of cyberbullying.

Sign 7: Dramatic Weight Loss or Weight Gain

When a teenager feels like they have lost total control over their lives, they can manifest their panic in other ways, like eating too much or eating too little. To them, eating becomes something they can actually control. Overeating can help them feel full and satisfied, while everything else feels like total isolation. Or eating disorders, like anorexia, can make them feel more appealing and desirable if the cyberbully called them fat.

There are enormous body pressures today with platforms like Instagram idolizing men and women that look like Barbie dolls. If your child doesn't fit the mold, they could be a victim of body shaming via the internet without you even realizing it.

Sign 8: Suicidal Thoughts or Attempts

This is such a difficult topic, but one that we must address to be comprehensive in our understanding of cyberbullying. We've already listed some instances in which kids ranging in age from ten to eighteen years old have taken their lives because of cyberbullying and outing.

If you notice your child is cutting themselves or if their therapist is alerting you to suicidal thoughts, this can be a major side effect of deeply engrained cyberbullying. Obviously, seek professional help immediately, and shut down all technological/social media connections if possible.

There are also other ways to determine if a child is being cyberbullied, like if they throw a phone or tablet against the wall after using it. When it comes down to it, common sense can tell you which behaviors might indicate your child is being cyberbullied. Constant vigilance will help you determine if you must take action.

CHAPTER 9

How to Know if Your Student Is Being Cyberbullied

It's more problematic for teachers to intervene with cyberbullying than it is for parents. However, teachers often spend more time with the student than the parent, which means they can have a critically important vantage point in the kind of bullying that occurs today.

Many cyberbullying cases continue on in person at school, especially if the student has been the victim of a mass text chain, etc. Teachers can pick up on the gossip, ridicule, and bullying right in their classroom and alert the school, administration, school psychologist, and, hopefully, the parents.

Here, teachers can be the most important component in the entire cyberbullying web. Therefore, if you are a teacher today, you know how much pressure you are under to serve your students to the best of your ability.

The following are a few tips that will make it a little easier for you.

8 Signs Your Student Is Being Cyberbullied

Sign 1: Removes Self from Classroom Chatter and Engagement

In most classrooms, there is a desk setup that faces the teacher at the front of the room. If you notice a student sitting in the very back, in isolation, even removing their desk from the rest of the layout, that can be a sign of a student under immense psychological duress. These students will also avoid group activities and talking to other students during downtime.

If the student used to be normal, engaging with some kids here and there, then their newfound isolation should be a clear indicator you should have a conversation with them.

Sign 2: Dramatic Mood Swings

As we have mentioned, mood swings are typical in teenagers. However, they shouldn't be tangible in a classroom setting. If you notice a student that cannot contain their mood swings and angry outbursts, going so far as to make a scene in front of everyone, that can be a sign they are a victim of cyberbullying (especially if these mood swings occur after they check their phone during class).

Sign 3: Work Ethic and Grades Drop

When one feels like the world is caving in on them, the last thing they care about is their grades. Especially if they are suffering from depression and anxiety, it can make studying for a test seem impossible.

Therefore, if a student is flunking dramatically, and perhaps never used to show such disinterest in school, it can be a sign they are detaching from the reality around them.

Sign 4: Skips Class Frequently

Victims of cyberbullies want to try to avoid contact with their classmates as much as possible. Maybe they've been outed or have had a seriously inappropriate photo texted around about them. Whatever happened, facing the recipients in person is absolutely mortifying.

Therefore, they will skip class whenever they can.

Sign 5: Disappears During Lunchtime

When it's time to sit down in the cafeteria and eat lunch with friends at school, a cyberbully victim might disappear. They may eat their lunch in the bathroom so no one can see them, or just walk the halls so they need not eat at all (eating disorder). This is why it's wise to check in on students during lunch and just observe their general behavior when possible.

Sign 6: Displays Obvious Depression Signs

If a student puts their head down during class to sleep, doesn't bring in any textbooks, or appears extremely sluggish and low energy, these are all visible signs of depression. Although you can't fix their depression singlehandedly, you can certainly ensure their parents and the school psychologist are made aware so the student can receive mental help and support.

Sign 7: Friend Changes

As a teacher, it's easy to detect which students are friends and which ones are not. Let's say you have a student start the school year in your class with four other friends. They are inseparable. They are so close you have to scold them about talking every now and then.

Well, fast-forward to March. You notice one of the friend group members has stopped sitting with the group. They have started to sit in the back, away from everyone, while their former friend group snickers at them. This student stops answering your questions, caring, or studying for tests.

The only other student they'll talk to is the other depressed student in the back. This is your red flag.

Sign 8: You Can Hear Students Mocking Them

As we have mentioned, you have a unique vantage point as a teacher. You can listen to the conversations in your classroom and out in the hallway. If a student has been a victim of a massive cyberbullying campaign, you will hear statements made about it between students in school. You should report this to the powers that be immediately, so the student can receive some help and encouragement.

Teaching is about more than helping students master a subject; it's about helping them grow and flourish into the people they were always meant to be. Cyberbullying can derail that along the way, which is why it's up to you to do something about it.

CHAPTER 10

7 Side Effects of Being Cyberbullied

It's time to dive a little deeper and look at the significant psychological side effects that happen to cyberbullying victims. Knowing these side effects can help you better determine if a child or student is in need and work on other ways to mitigate this problem in our society today. Everyone should know these side effects, even young teenagers that wonder why their friend no longer wants to hang out after school, etc.

Cyberbullying can make a victim feel like they are entirely alone. It can make them feel like they are worthless and unwanted, and that they are worthy of the onslaught of insults and psychological manipulation occurring through their phone every single day. It can alter their sense of reality and plunge their mind into mental sickness that is crippling, terrifying, and sometimes, conducive to suicidal thoughts.

And the scary thing is, this can happen to any student. Even if your child is captain of the football team, if his sexual orientation is made public against his will, it can ruin him and make him feel like the only person on the planet. As humans, we weren't made to feel alone. We were made to live in a community, with other people who support us.

Cyberbullying comes in and slashes that connected concept instantly. Therefore, the side effects can be alarming, hard to come to grips with, and sometimes, difficult to undo. But with support from friends and family and access to mental care services, we believe anything is possible.

Here are seven main side effects of being cyberbullied:

1. **Chronic Depression:**
   Approximately 20 percent of teenagers will experience depression before they reach adulthood today.[39] That's a staggering one-fifth of students that attend any school. That number is at an all-time high, which is why it's no secret that it's related to technology and the availability of social media.

   A student that is a victim of cyberbullying will develop chronic depression. The longer the bullying goes on, the worse the depression can become, as depression is the body's and brain's natural way of responding to something, completely ruining the target's life. As a student develops depression, other things come along for the ride, like trouble sleeping, anxiety, eating disorders, and even suicidal thoughts.

   Depression is no joke, which is why even adults can't seem to shake it or conquer it. Chronic depression can convince us of things our rational selves would never consider. It's a slippery slope, especially for a child so young.

2. **Anger and Vengeance:**
   When we are bullied, we have two options as a response: we can feel sad, isolated, and depressed, or we can feel angry, enraged, and filled with vengeance. Many victims will feel both feelings from time to time. As they feel this anger more and more frequently, it will make them an angry person.

   Holding onto anger won't do the victim's health any favors. Anger has been linked to increased anxiety, high blood pressure, and headaches.[40] And as the child matures into an adult carrying this anger, it can make them a meaner, angrier, and possibly abusive parent to the child they will rear in the future.

(In extreme cases, cyberbullying can make the victim violent as they seek revenge for the duress they have endured.)

3. **Low Self-Esteem:**
    Self-esteem is such an important psychological component to a teenager's brain. Without self-esteem, they are victims of everything from insults to body shaming. Self-esteem inspires us to keep going when it feels like the world is against us. It's what separates the good job candidates from the great ones—the inventors and the CEOs.

    No one will toot your horn for you in this life. You must be able to toot it yourself. That's why low self-esteem has such a degrading effect, one that will haunt the victim forever. It will convince them they are never worthy of anything good, from a dream job to a loving spouse.

4. **Poor Grades and Poor Education Options:**
    Regardless of the victim's natural intelligence levels, cyberbullying will make them depressed, tired, and unmotivated as they stay up late into the night, thinking dark thoughts. The victim will stop caring about school and, therefore, their grades. They will go from being an A or B student to just barely passing every class. This can have longer-term ramifications in life to include university acceptance chances.

5. **Self-Destructive Behavior:**
    Sometimes when we feel like we are caught in a bullying circle, we blame ourselves. We might think, "It's my fault that this happened. I shouldn't have taken that picture," or, "Well,

I did deserve to be made fun of because I am, in fact, ugly. They weren't wrong." We believe what we have been told because psychologically, it makes it all a little easier. We think we're deserving of the abuse, which can lead to self-harm, substance abuse, and other destructive behaviors that harm our health. This can lead victims to drug and alcohol addiction, eating disorders, and wrist cutting, and the list goes on.

6. **Increased Suicidal Thoughts:**
    Research shows that in 2017, there were 11.8 deaths per one hundred thousand adolescents ages fifteen to nineteen, which was up from 8 deaths per one hundred thousand in the year 2000.[41] The number is continuing to increase with each passing year and the availability of technology and social media today. It's definitely not a coincidence.

    Therefore, being bullied, silently, day after day, can cause the victim to develop suicidal thoughts. "What if I wasn't here anymore? Would anyone even notice? The bully says the world would be better off without me. Maybe they're right."

    We all cringed our way through the Michelle Carter case in which a teenage girlfriend continued to text her boyfriend and tell him to kill himself. He finally did, and she was sentenced to fifteen months in prison.[42]

    We are only so resilient. Taking a psychological beating every single day will convince the strongest of people to consider possibly taking their own life.

7. **Difficulty Establishing Trust:**
    Cyberbully victims often have a hard time believing that other people have good intentions since they have experienced the darker side of human nature repeatedly. Especially if the

victim was catfished, they don't necessarily know who they can believe, or if they really ever can trust again.

It's somewhat related to post-traumatic stress disorder (PTSD), which is very much a reality and a rational side effect for someone held mentally captive in a cyberbullying relationship.

Not trusting can affect friendships, the potential for romance and union, and other kinds of things, like networking for better jobs, etc.

The overall antisocial side effects of cyberbullying can strangle a victim for their entire lives, even if the bullying ensued for just one year. That's why it's so important to have dialogues and help the kids and students in your life feel like they can tell you what's going on. The longer cyberbullying occurs with no help, the more detrimental these side effects can become.

CHAPTER 11

5 Ways to Prevent Cyberbullying

So, can we all be more proactive in this fight? Do we just need to accept that cyberbullying is here to stay? Can we do something to protect our children from the horrors of psychological manipulation?

As a parent, you want to know how you can be proactive. You don't just want to sit by while your teen disappears down the social media rabbit hole with cyberbullying lurking over their shoulder. You want them back, present, and happy at the dinner table, with their phone in their pocket and their attitude in a positive place.

Well, we can't make Facebook or Instagram go away, but we can do a few things to help:

1. **Privatize Your Children's Accounts:**
   Facebook makes it easy for individuals to keep their profiles private today. Although you can't stop your kid from being on social media, you can sit down with them and request that their accounts be made extra private—so private that predators can't even look them up.

   That way, you can guarantee information won't get into the wrong hands. Your kid can also control who they allow to follow them, so if a notorious bully sends a request, they can decline it and go on with their day. This builds good habits on what can be made fully public, and what should not, which will have implications down the road for them. Driving home the idea that nothing is truly private on the internet is very important to help frame their understanding of the internet. If the data is online, even if you have your settings set to private, it can still be accessed and distributed. A friend can copy it or the server where it is housed can be hacked. When your child understands this, they understand the most essential pillar to cybersecurity.

This, of course, goes for passwords as well. It's usually a good rule of thumb to change passwords frequently (more than once a year), just in case hackers are trying to access their social media accounts.

2. **Establish Internet Times:**
   The internet is a rabbit hole for teenagers. Again, you can't stop them from using it—that will get them made fun of by their classmates. But you can introduce balance into their lives. You can say they can be on social media between 3:00 and 8:00 PM, but at 8 PM, it's family time until they go to bed. You can also state that before bed, they need to read, leaving their phones in the basket downstairs.

   Practice this same rule on vacations and other trips where phones can completely detach kids from reality. Allowing them to use the phone still will make them less likely to rebel against you. But limiting their time on it will show them there is more to life than the apps in their pocket.

3. **Go Over Content Marketing:**
   Kids have no grip on reality, as I mentioned earlier with the *theory of mind*, which is why they are much more likely than adults to share personal information and imagery online. Make sure you have conversations with them and teach them about what is and is not acceptable for online distribution.

They may moan and groan through the lesson, but in the end, they'll hear you and probably listen to the advice.

4. **Let Them Know It Happens to Everyone:**
   One of the most isolating things about cyberbullying is the feeling that it isn't happening to anyone else. This is not true, and you should let your kid know that. Let them know it can happen to anyone, and if it happens to them, it's not a sign they are weak or a target—they are just experiencing the norm. It will make them more likely to tell you if it does start.

5. **Bolster Their Self-Esteem:**
   As a parent or teacher, it's up to you to encourage your kid's self-esteem from a young age. Invest in your child when they are young, allowing them to play with the things they want to play with and encouraging their passions (even if they deviate from your idea of cool). The more self-confident your kid is by the time they reach their teens, the less likely they are to become a victim of this kind of aggression.

Conclusion

Unlike other common problems facing today's kids, cyberbullying is a complex issue with many different facets and techniques, and it changes with every new technological development. It's crucial that parents and teachers are aware of these different behaviors so they can help kids navigate the digital world and protect themselves. But what's most important is that kids learn the power of empathy.

Through empathy, they can put themselves in others' shoes and understand how their online behavior impacts others. The technology will continue to change. Social media will continue to grow. There will always be a bandwagon to jump on. But empathy remains unchanged. When it's used, it can inspire kindness and save lives. The power of empathy is constant, regardless of how the digital world is changing around us.

Cyberbullying has many root causes, and if we can solve for those, we can truly make a difference in online discourse and in the lives of our kids and all those they affect.

With that, we've reached the end of this educational journey. Congratulations! You are undoubtedly a cyberbullying expert, equipped with the tools and knowledge to keep everyone around you safer, more aware, and more protected in this digital age. To conquer the threat of cyberbullying, we must all be more vigilant, sharing education, tips, and insights with the other students, kids, parents, and teachers in our lives.

It's up to you to get out there and tell others about what you learned in this e-book.

Security Squad

Here at Security Squad, we leverage our CIA and intelligence expertise to make the world a safer place for you, your family, and our communities. We believe that instead of wishing away the world of technology, we should be accepting its arrival and changing our approach to keeping our kids and students safe.

That's where we come into the picture. You don't have to do it alone!

If you want to know more about cyberbullying, please get in contact with our team today.

Are you ready to join the movement?

References

"14 Signs of Cyberbullying in the Classroom." *CU Online*, 29 July 2019, https://online.campbellsville.edu/education/signs-of-cyberbullying/.

"51 Critical Cyber Bullying Statistics in 2019." *BroadbandSearch.net*, https://www.broadbandsearch.net/blog/cyber-bullying-statistics.

Emma. "Where Does Cyberbullying Happen?" *LearnSafe*, 27 Feb. 2018, https://learnsafe.com/where-does-cyberbullying-happen/.

"Four Things to Know About Cyberbullying." *NIDA for Teens*, NIDA, 20 Sept. 2016, https://teens.drugabuse.gov/blog/post/four-things-know-about-cyberbullying.

Gordon, Sherri. "6 Common Ways Kids Bully Online." *Verywell Family*, Verywell Family, 13 Sept. 2019, https://www.verywellfamily.com/types-of-cyberbullying-460549.

Gordon, Sherri. "8 Reasons Why Cyberbullies Lash Out at Others." *Verywell Family*, Verywell Family, 14 Aug. 2019, https://www.verywellfamily.com/reasons-why-kids-cyberbully-others-460553.

Hooker, Mara. "5 Ways to Prevent Cyber Bullying." *Net Nanny*, 28 Mar. 2016, https://www.netnanny.com/blog/5-ways-to-prevent-cyber-bullying/.

Hughes, Locke. "What Everyone Needs to Know About Cyberbullying." *WebMD*, WebMD, 21 Feb. 2017, https://www.webmd.com/a-to-z-guides/features/what-everyone-needs-to-know-about-cyberbullying.

Hurley, Katie. "Short Term and Long Term Effects of Bullying: Psychological & Societal." *Psycom.net - Mental Health Treatment Resource Since 1986*, 26 Sept. 2018, https://www.psycom.net/effects-of-bullying.

Nemours. "Cyberbullying: What You Need to Know." *Promise*, 22 Oct. 2018, http://blog.nemours.org/2018/10/cyberbullying-what-you-need-to-know/.

Parrack, Dave. "What Is the Imbecilic Art of Vaguebooking?" *MakeUseOf*, 15 Feb. 2012, https://www.makeuseof.com/tag/imbecilic-art-vaguebooking/.

"6 Signs Your Child Is Being Cyberbullied—and What to Do About It."
https://www.scholastic.com/parents/family-life/social-emotional-
learning/technology-and-kids/tackle-online-bullies.html.

Woda, Steven, and Jenny Evans. "10 Signs Your Child Is a Cyberbullying Victim."
UKnowKids Digital Parenting and Safety Blog, 27 Mar. 2019,
https://resources.uknowkids.com/blog/bid/173713/10-signs-your-child-is-a-
cyberbullying-victim.

---

[1] Anderson, Jenny. "Even Teens Are Worried They Spend Too Much Time on Their
Phones." Quartz, Quartz, 23 Aug. 2018, https://qz.com/1367506/pew-research-
teens-worried-they-spend-too-much-time-on-phones/.

[2] Rosenblatt, Kalhan. "Cyberbullying Tragedy: New Jersey Family to Sue After 12-
Year-Old Daughter's Suicide." NBCNews.com, NBC Universal News Group, 2 Aug.
2017, https://www.nbcnews.com/news/us-news/new-jersey-family-sue-school-
district-after-12-year-old-n788506.

[3] "51 Critical Cyber Bullying Statistics in 2019." BroadbandSearch.net,
https://www.broadbandsearch.net/blog/cyber-bullying-statistics.

[4] "51 Critical Cyber Bullying Statistics in 2019." BroadbandSearch.net,
https://www.broadbandsearch.net/blog/cyber-bullying-statistics.

[5] Anderson, Monica, and Jingjing Jiang. "Teens, Social Media & Technology 2018."
Pew Research Center: Internet, Science & Tech, Pew Research Center, 30 Nov.
2018, https://www.pewresearch.org/internet/2018/05/31/teens-social-media-
technology-2018/.

[6] Anderson, Monica, and Jingjing Jiang. "Teens, Social Media & Technology 2018."
Pew Research Center: Internet, Science & Tech, Pew Research Center, 30 Nov.
2018, https://www.pewresearch.org/internet/2018/05/31/teens-social-media-
technology-2018/.

[7] "Ditch the Label, Your World Prejudice Free: The Annual Bullying Survey 2017."
DitchtheLabel.org, Ditch the Label, July 2017, https://www.ditchthelabel.org/wp-
content/uploads/2017/07/The-Annual-Bullying-Survey-2017-1.pdf.

[8] Anderson, Monica, and Jingjing Jiang. "Teens, Social Media & Technology 2018." Pew Research Center: Internet, Science & Tech, Pew Research Center, 30 Nov. 2018, https://www.pewresearch.org/internet/2018/05/31/teens-social-media-technology-2018/.

[9] Public Affairs. "Facts About Bullying." StopBullying.gov, 18 Dec. 2019, https://www.stopbullying.gov/resources/facts#stats.

[10] Lenhart, Amanda. "Cyberbullying." Pew Research Center: Internet, Science & Tech, Pew Research Center, 27 June 2006, https://www.pewresearch.org/internet/2007/06/27/cyberbullying/.

[11] Public Affairs. "Laws, Policies & Regulations." StopBullying.gov, U.S. Department of Health and Human Services, 7 Jan. 2018, https://www.stopbullying.gov/resources/laws.

[12] Public Affairs. "Federal Laws." StopBullying.gov, U.S. Department of Health and Human Services, 26 Sept. 2017, https://www.stopbullying.gov/resources/laws/federal.

[13] Public Affairs. "Laws, Policies & Regulations." StopBullying.gov, U.S. Department of Health and Human Services, https://www.stopbullying.gov/

[14] "An Explanation of the Growing Phenomenon of Cyberbullying." National Crime Prevention Council, Bureau of Justice Assistance, Office of Justice Programs. U.S. Department of Justice, 2019, https://www.ncpc.org/resources/cyberbullying/what-is-cyberbullying/.

[15] "Ditch the Label, Your World Prejudice Free: The Annual Bullying Survey 2017." DitchtheLabel.org, Ditch the Label, July 2017, https://www.ditchthelabel.org/wp-content/uploads/2017/07/The-Annual-Bullying-Survey-2017-1.pdf.

[16] Lenhart, Amanda. "Teens, Technology and Friendships: Chapter 4: Social Media and Friendships." Pew Research Center: Internet, Science & Tech, Pew Research Center, 6 August 2015, https://www.pewresearch.org/internet/2015/08/06/chapter-4-social-media-and-friendships/.

[17] Curtin, Melanie. "Bill Gates Says This Is the 'Safest' Age to Give a Child a Smartphone." Inc.com, Inc., 10 May 2017, https://www.inc.com/melanie-curtin/bill-gates-says-this-is-the-safest-age-to-give-a-child-a-smartphone.html.

[18] Gordon, Sherri. "5 Myths About Victims of Bullying." Verywell Family, 26 Oct. 2019, https://www.verywellfamily.com/myths-about-victims-of-bullying-460781.

[19] Witchalls, Clint. "Why a Lack of Empathy Is the Root of All Evil." The Independent, Independent Digital News and Media, 19 Dec. 2011, https://www.independent.co.uk/life-style/health-and-families/features/why-a-lack-of-empathy-is-the-root-of-all-evil-6279239.html.

[20] Sheltzer, Leo F. "Cold People: What Makes Them That Way? Part 1." Psychology Today, Sussex Publishers, 31 May 2011, https://www.psychologytoday.com/us/blog/évolution-the-self/201105/cold-people-what-makes-them-way-part-1.

[21] Rymanowicz, Kylie, and Michigan State University. "Monkey See, Monkey Do: Model Behavior in Early Childhood." Michigan State University, 30 Mar. 2015, https://www.canr.msu.edu/news/monkey_see_monkey_do_model_behavior_in_early_childhood.

[22] "Is Making a Threat on Social Media a Crime?" PBS, Public Broadcasting Service, 2 Dec. 2014, https://www.pbs.org/newshour/extra/daily-videos/is-making-a-threat-on-social-media-a-crime/.

[23] "Facts and Case Summary - Elonis v. U.S." United States Courts, 2015, https://www.uscourts.gov/educational-resources/educational-activities/facts-and-case-summary-elonis-v-us.

[24] Meyer, Robinson. "The Primary Way to Report Harassment on the Social Web Is Broken." The Atlantic, Atlantic Media Company, 21 Aug. 2014, https://www.theatlantic.com/technology/archive/2014/08/the-way-we-report-harassment-on-the-social-web-is-broken/378730/.

[25] "Harassing Text Messages." Crime Scene, https://www.crimescene.com/casefiles-doc/2074-evidence-texts.

[26] Fitzsimons, Tim. "Tennessee Teen's Suicide Highlights Dangers of Anti-LGBTQ Bullying." NBCNews.com, NBC Universal News Group, 1 Oct. 2019, https://www.nbcnews.com/feature/nbc-out/tennessee-teen-s-suicide-highlights-dangers-anti-lgbtq-bullying-n1060976.

[27] Aviles, Gwen. "Nearly 2 Million LGBTQ Youths Contemplate Suicide Each Year." NBCNews.com, NBC Universal News Group, 28 June 2019, https://www.nbcnews.com/feature/nbc-out/nearly-2-million-lgbtq-youths-contemplate-suicide-each-year-n1023461.

[28] Reuters. "One in Four Pre-Teen Suicides May Be LGBTQ Youth." NBCNews.com, NBC Universal News Group, 22 Feb. 2019, https://www.nbcnews.com/feature/nbc-out/one-four-pre-teen-suicides-may-be-lgbtq-youth-n974481.

[29] "Tyler Clementi Higher Education Anti-Harassment Act of 2019." U.S. Congress, U.S. Senate, 2019, https://www.help.senate.gov/imo/media/doc/Tyler Clementi Higher Education Anti-Harassment Act Fact Sheet FINAL.pdf.

[30] Parker, Lara. "17 Of The Most Insane Catfish Stories That Will Make You Cringe." BuzzFeed, BuzzFeed, 3 June 2015, https://www.buzzfeed.com/laraparker/insane-catfish-stories-that-will-make-you-want-to-delete.

[31] Tomasello, Michael. "How Children Come to Understand False Beliefs: A Shared Intentionality Account." PNAS, National Academy of Sciences, 21 Aug. 2018, https://www.pnas.org/content/115/34/8491.

[32] Hansen, Mikkel B. "If You Know Something, Say Something: Young Children's Problem with False Beliefs." Frontiers in Psychology, Frontiers Research Foundation, 5 July 2010, https://www.ncbi.nlm.nih.gov/pmc/articles/PMC3176414/.

[33] "Sex Offenders Map." National Center for Missing & Exploited Children (NCMEC), National Center for Missing & Exploited Children (NCMEC), 24 May 2017, https://api.missingkids.org/en_US/documents/Sex_Offenders_Map.pdf.

[34] Barr, Luke. "FBI Warns Parents 'Sextortion' Cases Involving Children on the Rise." ABC News, ABC News Network, 3 June 2019, https://abcnews.go.com/Politics/fbi-warns-parents-sextortion-cases-involving-children-rise/story?id=63450973.

[35] Kashner, Sam. "Exclusive: Jennifer Lawrence Speaks About Her Stolen Photos." Vanity Fair, 20 Oct. 2014, https://www.vanityfair.com/hollywood/2014/10/jennifer-lawrence-photo-hacking-privacy.

[36] "Real Life Examples of Cyber-Bullying - Cease Cyber-Bullying." Google Sites, https://sites.google.com/a/cypanthers.org/cease-cyber-bullying/real-life-examples-of-cyber-bullying.

[37] Schocket, Ryan. "17 Times Celebs Subtweeted The Crap Out Of Each Other." BuzzFeed.com, BuzzFeed, 22 May 2018, https://www.buzzfeed.com/ryanschocket2/17-times-celebs-subtweeted-the-shit-out-of-each-other.

[38] Campbell, Denis. "Facebook and Twitter 'Harm Young People's Mental Health'." The Guardian, Guardian News and Media, 19 May 2017, https://www.theguardian.com/society/2017/may/19/popular-social-media-sites-harm-young-peoples-mental-health.

[39] Borchard, Therese J. "Why Are So Many Teens Depressed?" World of Psychology, 8 July 2018, https://psychcentral.com/blog/why-are-so-many-teens-depressed/.

[40] Department of Health & Human Services. "Anger - How It Affects People." Better Health Channel, Department of Health & Human Services, 31 Jan. 2014, https://www.betterhealth.vic.gov.au/health/healthyliving/anger-how-it-affects-people.

[41] Frazee, Gretchen, and Patty Gorena Morales. "Suicide among Teens and Young Adults Reaches Highest Level since 2000." PBS, Public Broadcasting Service, 18 June 2019, https://www.pbs.org/newshour/nation/suicide-among-teens-and-young-adults-reaches-highest-level-since-2000.

[42] Frazee, Gretchen, and Patty Gorena Morales. "Suicide among Teens and Young Adults Reaches Highest Level since 2000." PBS, Public Broadcasting Service, 18 June 2019, https://www.pbs.org/newshour/nation/suicide-among-teens-and-young-adults-reaches-highest-level-since-2000.